The Shanghai Maths Project

For the English National Curriculum

G000295834

Year 3 Learning

William Collins' dream of knowledge for all began with the publication of his first book in 1819.

A self-educated mill worker, he not only enriched millions of lives, but also founded a flourishing publishing house. Today, staying true to this spirit, Collins books are packed with inspiration, innovation and practical expertise. They place you at the centre of a world of possibility and give you exactly what you need to explore it.

Collins. Freedom to teach.

Published by Collins
An imprint of HarperCollins*Publishers*
The News Building
1 London Bridge Street
London
SE1 9GF

MIX
Paper from responsible sources
FSC
www.fsc.org
FSC™ C007454

This book is produced from independently certified FSC paper to ensure responsible forest management.

For more information visit:
www.harpercollins.co.uk/green

Browse the complete Collins catalogue at
www.collins.co.uk

© HarperCollins*Publishers* Limited 2017

10 9 8 7 6 5 4 3 2 1

978-0-00-822597-1

Learning Books Series Editor: Amanda Simpson

Practice Books Series Editor: Professor Lianghuo Fan

Authors: Caroline Clissold, Sarah Eaton, Linda Glithro, Jane Jones, Steph King, Brian Macdonald, Cherri Moseley, Richard Perring, Paul Wrangles

British Library Cataloguing in Publication Data

A catalogue record for this publication is available from the British Library.

Publishing Manager: Fiona McGlade
In-house Editor: Nina Smith
In-house Editorial Assistant: August Stevens
Project Manager: Emily Hooton
Copy Editors: Jane Wood
Proofreaders: Tony Clappison and Steven Matchett
Cover design: Kevin Robbins and East China Normal University Press Ltd
Cover artwork: Daniela Geremia
Internal design: Amparo Barrera
Typesetting: Ken Vail Graphic Design and 2Hoots Publishing Services Ltd
Illustrations: Matt Ward (Beehive Illustration)
Production: Rachel Weaver

Printed and bound by Grafica Veneta, S.p.A., Italy

Photo acknowledgements
The publishers wish to thank the following for permission to reproduce photographs. Every effort has been made to trace copyright holders and to obtain their permission for the use of copyright materials. The publishers will gladly receive any information enabling them to rectify any error or omission at the first opportunity.

(t = top, c = centre, b = bottom, r = right, l = left)

p28 t Fouad A. Saad/Shutterstock, p28 c iunewind/Shutterstock, p32 l Aleksandr Bryliaev/ Shutterstock, p33 tr illpos/Shutterstock, p35 tr Aleksandr Bryliaev/Shutterstock, p38 c Viktoriya Yakubouskaya/Shutterstock, p40 tc Aleksandr Bryliaev/Shutterstock, p42 br Plan-B/ Shutterstock, p44 c Jemastock/Shutterstock

Bar models

Bar models can show the relationship between the whole and its parts.

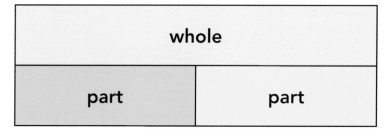

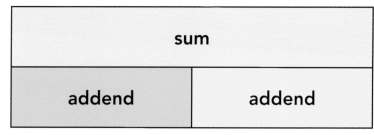

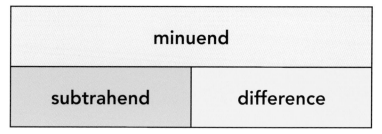

Line models

Line models also show the relationship between the whole and its parts.

Sometimes the whole is at the bottom and sometimes at the top.

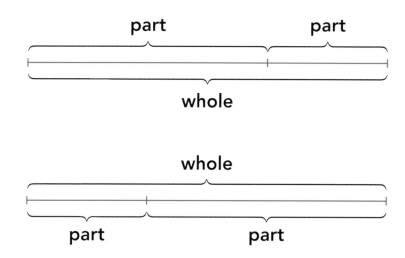

Comparing parts using a bar model

Bar models can show how different parts compare with each other.
How many more cars are there than vans?

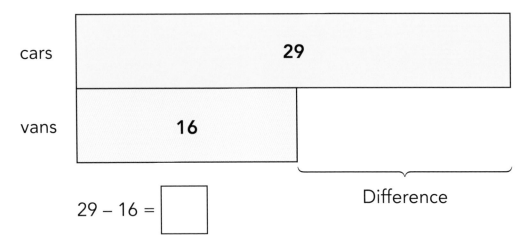

29 − 16 = ☐

Difference

The same bar models can help solve problems to find unknown sums.

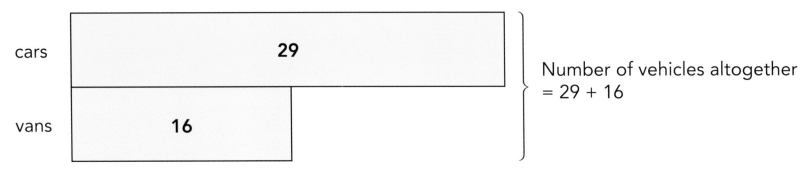

Number of vehicles altogether
= 29 + 16

Comparing parts using a line model

Line models show the same information as bar models.

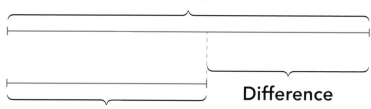

29 – 16 = ☐

Ten frame

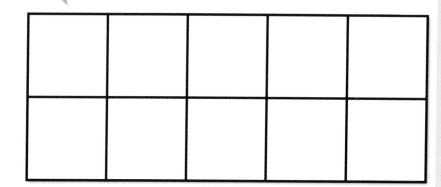

Number bonds for 10

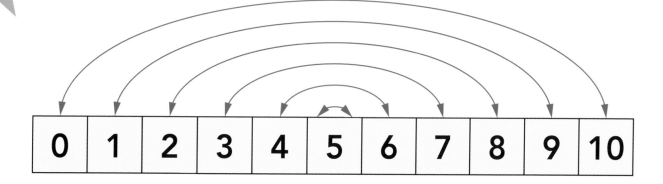

Array

4 × 3 = 12
3 × 4 = 12
12 ÷ 3 = 4
12 ÷ 4 = 3

Multiplication and division fact family

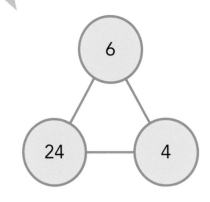

6 × 4 = 24
4 × 6 = 24
24 ÷ 6 = 4
24 ÷ 4 = 6

The language of multiplication and division

factor × factor = product
dividend ÷ divisor = quotient

Multiplication grid

1 × 1 = 1									
1 × 2 = 2	2 × 2 = 4								
1 × 3 = 3	2 × 3 = 6	3 × 3 = 9							
1 × 4 = 4	2 × 4 = 8	3 × 4 = 12	4 × 4 = 16						
1 × 5 = 5	2 × 5 = 10	3 × 5 = 15	4 × 5 = 20	5 × 5 = 25					
1 × 6 = 6	2 × 6 = 12	3 × 6 = 18	4 × 6 = 24	5 × 6 = 30	6 × 6 = 36				
1 × 7 = 7	2 × 7 = 14	3 × 7 = 21	4 × 7 = 28	5 × 7 = 35	6 × 7 = 42	7 × 7 = 49			
1 × 8 = 8	2 × 8 = 16	3 × 8 = 24	4 × 8 = 32	5 × 8 = 40	6 × 8 = 48	7 × 8 = 56	8 × 8 = 64		
1 × 9 = 9	2 × 9 = 18	3 × 9 = 27	4 × 9 = 36	5 × 9 = 45	6 × 9 = 54	7 × 9 = 63	8 × 9 = 72	9 × 9 = 81	
1 × 10 = 10	2 × 10 = 20	3 × 10 = 30	4 × 10 = 40	5 × 10 = 50	6 × 10 = 60	7 × 10 = 70	8 × 10 = 80	9 × 10 = 90	10 × 10 = 100
1 × 11 = 11	2 × 11 = 22	3 × 11 = 33	4 × 11 = 44	5 × 11 = 55	6 × 11 = 66	7 × 11 = 77	8 × 11 = 88	9 × 11 = 99	10 × 11 = 110
1 × 12 = 12	2 × 12 = 24	3 × 12 = 36	4 × 12 = 48	5 × 12 = 60	6 × 12 = 72	7 × 12 = 84	8 × 12 = 96	9 × 12 = 108	10 × 12 = 120

Bar model showing multiplication and division

3	3	3	3	3	3
18					

$3 \times 6 = 18$

$18 \div 3 = 6$

Repeated addition on a number line

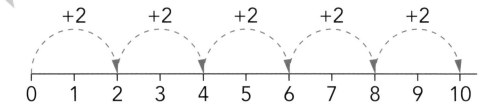

Arrays

This array represents:

$6 \times 7 = 42$

$7 \times 6 = 42$

$42 \div 7 = 6$

$42 \div 6 = 7$

Arrays with an additional part column or row

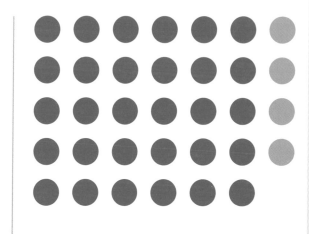

$6 \times 5 + 4 = 34$

$5 \times 6 + 4 = 34$

Multiplication and division families

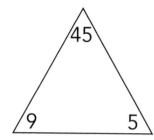

$9 \times 5 = 45$ $5 \times 9 = 45$ $45 \div 5 = 9$ $45 \div 9 = 5$

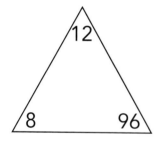

$8 \times 12 = 96$ $12 \times 8 = 96$ $96 \div 12 = 8$ $96 \div 8 = 12$

Making equal groups and sharing are both ways of dividing

$12 \div 4 = 3$

There are three groups of four in twelve.

If you share twelve things between four people they will have three things each.

Division with remainders

5

3

15

4

19

$19 \div 5 = 3 \text{ r } 4$

One more cabbage is needed to make another group of five.

19 cannot be divided equally by 5.

There is a remainder of 4.

Representing numbers

Here is the number **three hundred and seventy-two** represented in different ways.

$$372 = 300 + 70 + 2$$

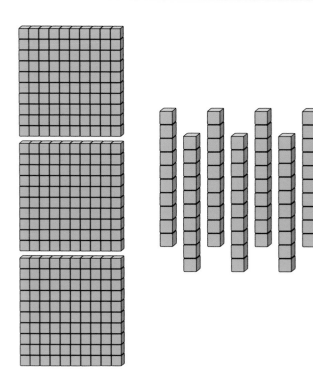

place value arrow cards

Hundreds	Tens	Ones
●●●	●●●●●●●	●●

370   **372**   380

Hundreds	Tens	Ones
3	7	2

Tables and bar charts

The results of a survey showing how Year 3 pupils at New School travel to school are shown in a table and in a bar chart.

Type of travel	Bus	Car	Scooter	Walking
Number of pupils	10	16	22	12

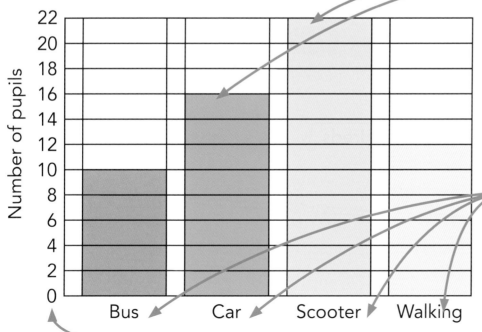

Bar chart showing how Year 3 pupils at New School travel to school

Scooter ... car ... I can see there are 3 cells more who travel by scooter – that's 6 more children.

Bus, car, scooter and walking – altogether, this is the number of pupils in Year 3.

Each cell represents 2 pupils.

Telling the time

minute hand

hour hand

How long is ... ?

60 minutes	is the same as	1 hour
24 hours	is the same as	1 day
7 days	is the same as	1 week
12 months	is the same as	1 year
common year	is the same as	365 days
leap year	is the same as	366 days

Common years and leap years

2019 – a common year:
28 days in February

2019 Calendar

January 2019	February 2019	March 2019	April 2019
S M T W T F S	S M T W T F S	S M T W T F S	S M T W T F S
1 2 3 4 5	1 2	1 2	1 2 3 4 5 6
6 7 8 9 10 11 12	3 4 5 6 7 8 9	3 4 5 6 7 8 9	7 8 9 10 11 12 13
13 14 15 16 17 18 19	10 11 12 13 14 15 16	10 11 12 13 14 15 16	14 15 16 17 18 19 20
20 21 22 23 24 25 26	17 18 19 20 21 22 23	17 18 19 20 21 22 23	21 22 23 24 25 26 27
27 28 29 30 31	24 25 26 27 28	24 25 26 27 28 29 30 / 31	28 29 30

May 2019	June 2019	July 2019	August 2019
S M T W T F S	S M T W T F S	S M T W T F S	S M T W T F S
1 2 3 4	1	1 2 3 4 5 6	1 2 3
5 6 7 8 9 10 11	2 3 4 5 6 7 8	7 8 9 10 11 12 13	4 5 6 7 8 9 10
12 13 14 15 16 17 18	9 10 11 12 13 14 15	14 15 16 17 18 19 20	11 12 13 14 15 16 17
19 20 21 22 23 24 25	16 17 18 19 20 21 22	21 22 23 24 25 26 27	18 19 20 21 22 23 24
26 27 28 29 30 31	23 24 25 26 27 28 29 / 30	28 29 30 31	25 26 27 28 29 30 31

September 2019	October 2019	November 2019	December 2019
S M T W T F S	S M T W T F S	S M T W T F S	S M T W T F S
1 2 3 4 5 6 7	1 2 3 4 5	1 2	1 2 3 4 5 6 7
8 9 10 11 12 13 14	6 7 8 9 10 11 12	3 4 5 6 7 8 9	8 9 10 11 12 13 14
15 16 17 18 19 20 21	13 14 15 16 17 18 19	10 11 12 13 14 15 16	15 16 17 18 19 20 21
22 23 24 25 26 27 28	20 21 22 23 24 25 26	17 18 19 20 21 22 23	22 23 24 25 26 27 28
29 30	27 28 29 30 31	24 25 26 27 28 29 30	29 30 31

2020 – a leap year:
29 days in February

2020 Calendar

January 2020	February 2020	March 2020	April 2020
S M T W T F S	S M T W T F S	S M T W T F S	S M T W T F S
1 2 3 4	1	1 2 3 4 5 6 7	1 2 3 4
5 6 7 8 9 10 11	2 3 4 5 6 7 8	8 9 10 11 12 13 14	5 6 7 8 9 10 11
12 13 14 15 16 17 18	9 10 11 12 13 14 15	15 16 17 18 19 20 21	12 13 14 15 16 17 18
19 20 21 22 23 24 25	16 17 18 19 20 21 22	22 23 24 25 26 27 28	19 20 21 22 23 24 25
26 27 28 29 30 31	23 24 25 26 27 28 29	29 30 31	26 27 28 29 30

May 2020	June 2020	July 2020	August 2020
S M T W T F S	S M T W T F S	S M T W T F S	S M T W T F S
1 2	1 2 3 4 5 6	1 2 3 4	1
3 4 5 6 7 8 9	7 8 9 10 11 12 13	5 6 7 8 9 10 11	2 3 4 5 6 7 8
10 11 12 13 14 15 16	14 15 16 17 18 19 20	12 13 14 15 16 17 18	9 10 11 12 13 14 15
17 18 19 20 21 22 23	21 22 23 24 25 26 27	19 20 21 22 23 24 25	16 17 18 19 20 21 22
24 25 26 27 28 29 30 / 31	28 29 30	26 27 28 29 30 31	23 24 25 26 27 28 29 / 30 31

September 2020	October 2020	November 2020	December 2020
S M T W T F S	S M T W T F S	S M T W T F S	S M T W T F S
1 2 3 4 5	1 2 3	1 2 3 4 5 6 7	1 2 3 4 5
6 7 8 9 10 11 12	4 5 6 7 8 9 10	8 9 10 11 12 13 14	6 7 8 9 10 11 12
13 14 15 16 17 18 19	11 12 13 14 15 16 17	15 16 17 18 19 20 21	13 14 15 16 17 18 19
20 21 22 23 24 25 26	18 19 20 21 22 23 24	22 23 24 25 26 27 28	20 21 22 23 24 25 26
27 28 29 30	25 26 27 28 29 30 31	29 30	27 28 29 30 31

a.m. and p.m.

a.m. is a time between midnight and noon.

p.m. is a time between noon and midnight.

Analogue and digital

When we tell the time we use analogue and digital clocks.

Digital clocks use either 12-hour or 24-hour times.

The 24-hour clock

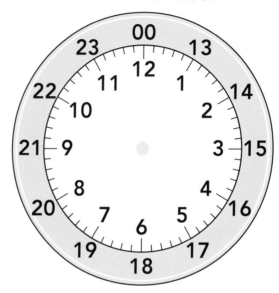

1.

16 minutes past 3

3:16

15:16

2.

25 minutes to 9

8:35

20:35

3.

24 minutes past 6

6:24

18:24

4.

3 minutes to 10

9:57

21:57

Using columns

353 + 148   772 − 259

```
    3 5 3          7 7 2
  + 1 4 8        − 2 5 9
  ─────────      ─────────
```

```
    3 5 3          7 ⁶7̸ ¹2
  + 1 4 8        − 2 5 9
  ─────────      ─────────
        1                3
      ₁
```

```
    3 5 3          7 ⁶7̸ ¹2
  + 1 4 8        − 2 5 9
  ─────────      ─────────
      0 1              1 3
    ₁   ₁
```

```
    3 5 3          7 ⁶7̸ ¹2
  + 1 4 8        − 2 5 9
  ─────────      ─────────
    5 0 1          5 1 3
    ₁   ₁
```

Partitioning

A number can be split up to make it easier to work with.

253 + 129 =

253 + 100 = 353

353 + 20 = 373

373 + 9 = 382

```
┌───┬───┬───┐
│ 1 │ 2 │ 9 │
└───┴───┴───┘

┌───────────┐
│ 1 0 0     │
└───────────┘

┌─────┐
│ 2 0 │
└─────┘

┌───┐
│ 9 │
└───┘
```

Regrouping

A number can be regrouped to help subtract from it.

483

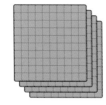

'Four hundred and seventy and thirteen' is the same as 483.

400   70   13

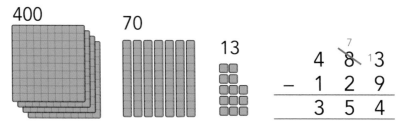

```
      4 8̸ ⁷¹3
    − 1 2 9
    ─────────
      3 5 4
```

Names of parts of calculations

Operation   Equals

Addend   Addend   Answer

$$250 + 70 = 320$$

Add   Total
Plus   Altogether
         Sum

Operation   Equals

Minuend   Subtrahend   Answer

$$460 - 50 = 410$$

Subtract   Difference
Take away
Minus

Rounding numbers

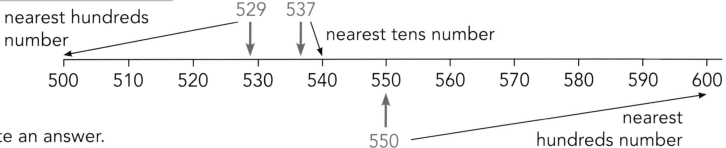

nearest hundreds number

529   537

nearest tens number

500   510   520   530   540   550   560   570   580   590   600

550

nearest hundreds number

Estimate an answer.
Round the numbers to the nearest ten …
$367 + 221 = \quad \rightarrow \quad 370 + 220 = 590$

… or to the nearest hundred.
$367 + 221 = \quad \rightarrow \quad 400 + 200 = 600$

Calculate the actual answer.

$$
\begin{array}{r}
3\ 6\ 7 \\
+\ 2\ 2\ 1 \\
\hline
5\ 8\ 8 \\
\end{array}
$$

19

Fraction language

How many parts of an object, quantity or number have been selected

$$\frac{Numerator}{Denominator}$$

How many equal parts an object, quantity or number has been divided into

$$\frac{2}{6}$$

2 parts of the object, quantity or number have been selected

The object, quantity or number has been divided into 6 equal parts

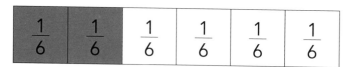

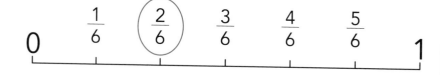

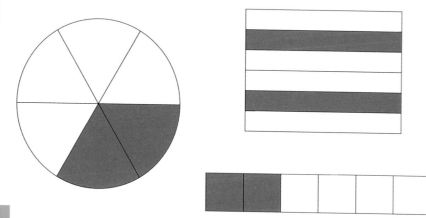

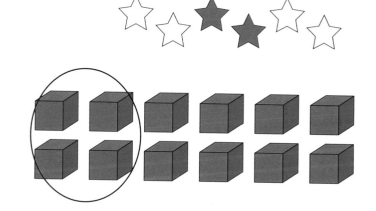

Equivalent fractions

Tenths

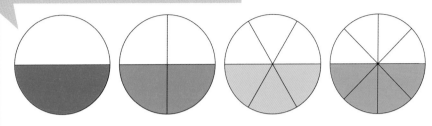

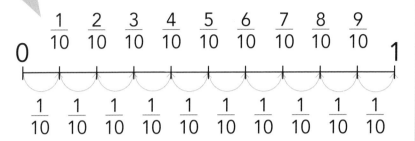

Five tenths is equivalent to one half

$$\frac{5}{10} = \frac{1}{2}$$

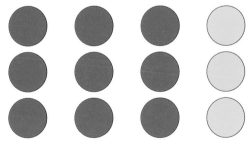

Nine twelfths is equivalent to three quarters

$$\frac{9}{12} = \frac{3}{4}$$

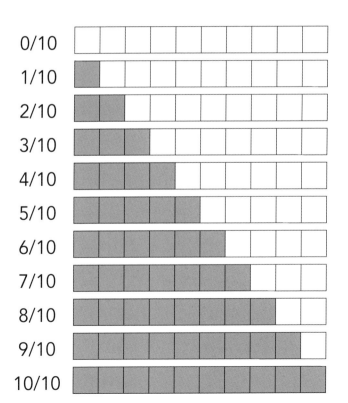

Adding and subtracting fractions

| $\frac{1}{5}$ | $\frac{1}{5}$ | $\frac{1}{5}$ | $\frac{1}{5}$ | $\frac{1}{5}$ |

$$\frac{1}{5} + \frac{4}{5} = \frac{5}{5}$$
$$\frac{5}{5} - \frac{1}{5} = \frac{4}{5}$$

| $\frac{1}{5}$ | $\frac{1}{5}$ | $\frac{1}{5}$ | $\frac{1}{5}$ | $\frac{1}{5}$ |

$$\frac{2}{5} + \frac{3}{5} = \frac{5}{5}$$
$$\frac{5}{5} - \frac{2}{5} = \frac{3}{5}$$

| $\frac{1}{5}$ | $\frac{1}{5}$ | $\frac{1}{5}$ | $\frac{1}{5}$ | $\frac{1}{5}$ |

$$\frac{3}{5} + \frac{2}{5} = \frac{5}{5}$$
$$\frac{5}{5} - \frac{3}{5} = \frac{2}{5}$$

| $\frac{1}{5}$ | $\frac{1}{5}$ | $\frac{1}{5}$ | $\frac{1}{5}$ | $\frac{1}{5}$ |

$$\frac{4}{5} + \frac{1}{5} = \frac{5}{5}$$
$$\frac{5}{5} - \frac{4}{5} = \frac{1}{5}$$

| $\frac{1}{5}$ | $\frac{1}{5}$ | $\frac{1}{5}$ | $\frac{1}{5}$ | $\frac{1}{5}$ |

$$\frac{5}{5} + \frac{0}{5} = \frac{5}{5}$$
$$\frac{5}{5} - \frac{5}{5} = \frac{0}{5}$$

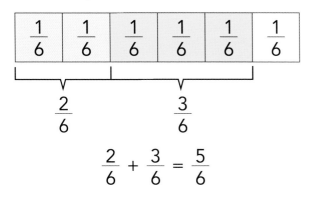

$$\frac{2}{6} + \frac{3}{6} = \frac{5}{6}$$

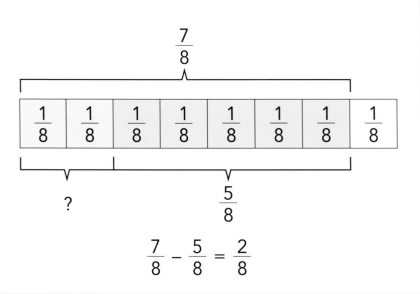

$$\frac{7}{8} - \frac{5}{8} = \frac{2}{8}$$

Multiplying by a number of tens or hundreds

3 ones

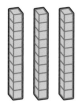

3 tens

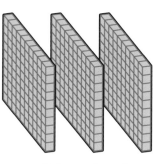

3 hundreds

$2 \times 3 = 6$

2 × 3 ones is 6 ones

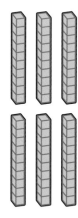

$2 \times 30 = 60$

2 × 3 tens is 6 tens

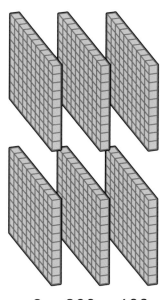

$2 \times 300 = 600$

2 × 3 hundreds is 6 hundreds

Written multiplication methods

Two ways to record 'Finding part products and adding them together'.

Method 1

34×6

$30 \times 6 = 180$

$4 \times 6 = 24$

$180 + 24 = 204$

So $34 \times 6 = 204$

Method 2

$$\begin{array}{r} 3\,4 \\ \times\ \ 6 \\ \hline 2\,4 \\ 1\,8\,0 \\ \hline 2\,0\,4 \\ \hline \end{array} \qquad \begin{array}{r} 3\,4 \\ \times\ \ 6 \\ \hline 2\,0\,4 \\ \hline \end{array}$$

The 2 tens in the product 24 has been written in the tens column.

Representing division

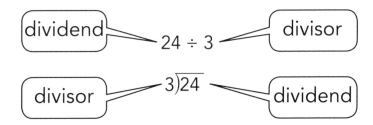

How many 3s are there in 24?

What is 24 shared equally between 3?

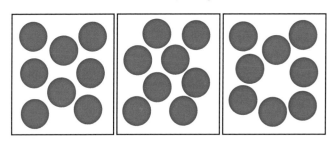

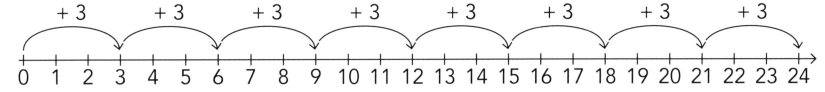

The relationship between division and multiplication

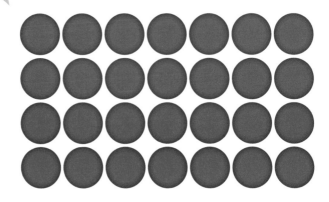

This array shows that:

$7 \times 4 = 28$

$4 \times 7 = 28$

$28 \div 4 = 7$

$28 \div 7 = 4$

The column method

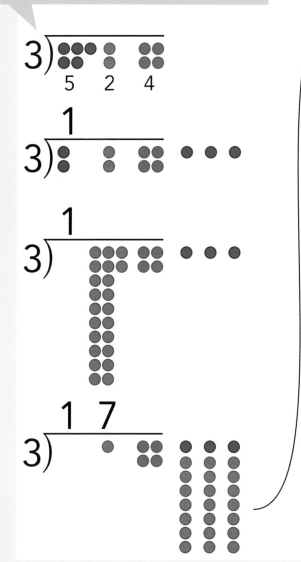

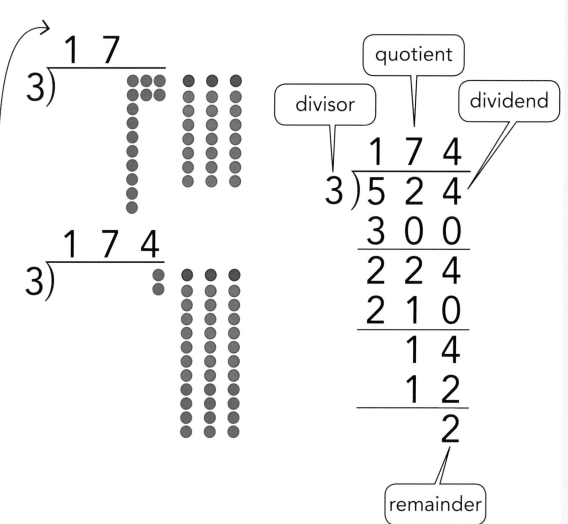

Tools for measuring length

We use rulers and metre sticks to measure how long things are.

Metre sticks show how many centimetres something measures.

We can measure small items accurately with a ruler.
Rulers show millimetres and centimetres.

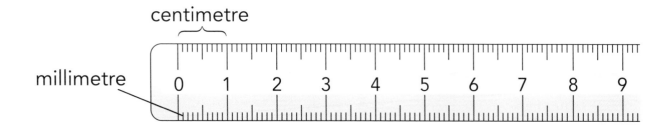

Comparing millimetres and centimetres and metres

10 millimetres	is the same as	1 centimetre
100 centimetres	is the same as	1 metre

Perimeter

The perimeter is the distance around the outside of a shape.

Imagine Perry the insect walking around the edge of the shape.

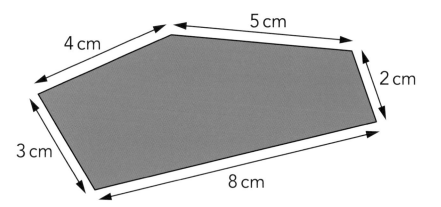

The perimeter of this pentagon is:
3 cm + 4 cm + 5 cm + 2 cm + 8 cm = 22 cm.

Angles

an acute angle

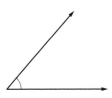

An acute angle is smaller than a right angle.

a right angle

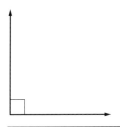

A right angle measures 90 degrees.

an obtuse angle

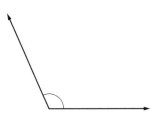

An obtuse angle is bigger than a right angle but smaller than a straight angle.

Lines

A vertical line runs straight up and down from top to bottom or bottom to top.

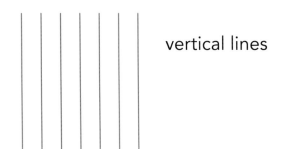

vertical lines

A horizontal line runs straight from right to left or left to right.

horizontal lines

Perpendicular lines are lines that meet or intersect at right angles.

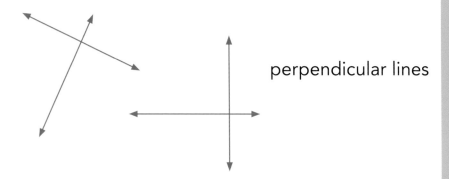

perpendicular lines

Parallel lines are lines that will never meet. They stay the same distance apart from each other.

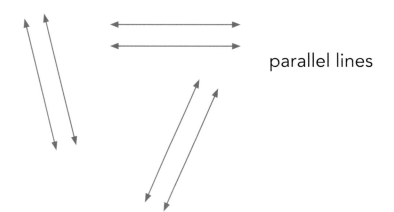

parallel lines

Making 3-D shapes from 2-D shapes

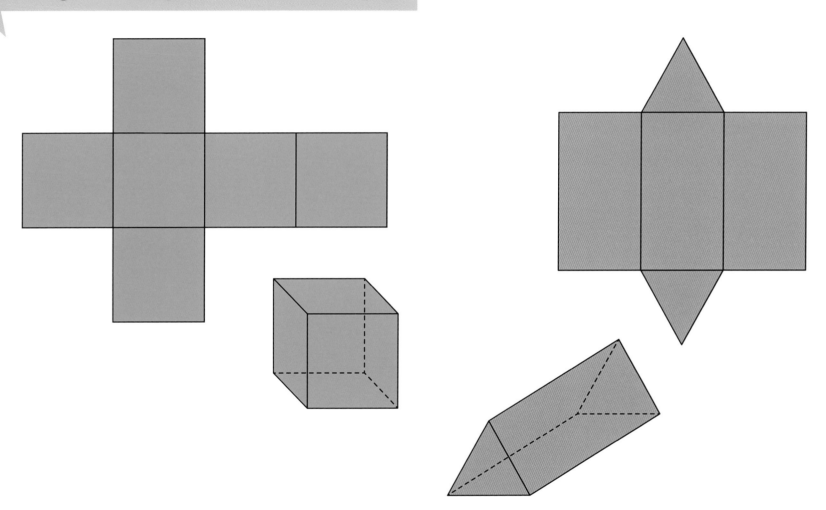

12-hour time: time is displayed as 00:00a.m. to 11:59a.m. for midnight to noon, and 12:00p.m. to 11:59p.m. for noon to midnight

24-hour time: time is displayed as 00:00 to 23:59 hours

a.m.: abbreviation for times between midnight and noon

acute angle: An angle that is smaller than a right angle. It is greater than 0 degrees and less than 90 degrees.

add, addition: Join or put together two or more numbers or values. The symbol for add is +.

addend: the number being added, or added to, in an addition calculation, addend + addend = sum

$$4 + 3 = 7$$

addends

analogue time: time shown using the hands on a clock

angle: the amount of turn between two straight lines that meet at a point

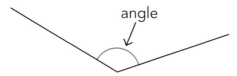

angle

answer: the result of a calculation

anticlockwise: in the opposite direction to the way the hands of a clock move

approximately: close to, roughly

array: a regular pattern of rows and columns for arranging symbols or objects

balanced: one side is the same as the other in some way

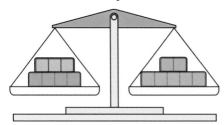

bar: a column or rectangle

bar chart: a display of data in which the height of each bar relates to the number of items

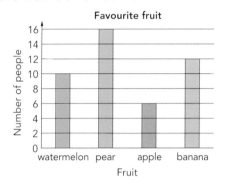

bar model: a diagram to show part–whole relationships

9	
4	5

base 10 blocks: mathematical blocks used to help understand place value

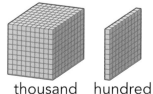

thousand   hundred   ten   one

block diagram: a diagram in which information is shown in blocks or as coloured squares

5			
4			
3			
2			
1			
	ladybirds	beetles	ants

boundary: a line marking the limit of an area

bracket: a symbol used to contain a group

( )

calculate: work out the answer to a question about numbers

calculation: a question about numbers written as a number sentence

$3 + 6 = 9, 7 - 2 = 5$

calendar: a table showing the days, weeks and months of a year

2019 Calendar

cell: a single rectangle or square in a block diagram

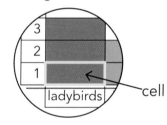

ladybirds   cell

centimetre (cm): a small unit of length; there are 100 centimetres in a metre

check: work something out again to make sure it makes sense and is correct

circle: a closed 2-D shape with one curved outline consisting of points that are the same distance from the centre

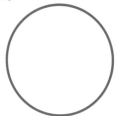

clockwise: in the direction that the hands of a clock move

column: a vertical arrangement of numbers or objects, or a shaded vertical block

$$\begin{array}{r} 5\ 7 \\ +\ 3\ 7 \\ \hline 9\ 4 \end{array}$$

column method: a formal written method of adding or subtracting in which the numbers are written vertically, according to the place value of each digit

$$\begin{array}{r} 5\ 6\ 7 \\ -\ 2\ 3\ 1 \\ \hline 3\ 3\ 6 \end{array}$$

common year: a year that has 365 days, not a leap year

2019 CALENDAR

JANUARY	FEBRUARY	MARCH	APRIL
MAY	JUNE	JULY	AUGUST
SEPTEMBER	OCTOBER		DECEMBER

commutative: a law for addition and multiplication that means the numbers can be swapped around without changing the answer

$5 + 3 = 8$ is the same as $3 + 5 = 8$

compensation: a mental calculation strategy in which a number is rounded to the nearest 10 to make the calculation easier, and the amount rounded up or down is compensated for at the end for example, $34 + 19 = \ldots$

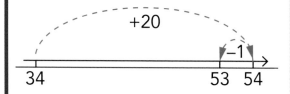

cone: a 3-D object with a circular base joined to a curved side that ends in a point

consecutive (numbers): numbers that follow each other in order, without gaps

6, 7, 8 are consecutive numbers

cube: a 3-D shape with 6 identical square faces, 12 edges and 8 vertices

cuboid: a 3-D shape with 6 rectangular faces, 2 of which might be square, 12 edges and 8 vertices

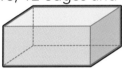

cylinder: a 3-D shape with two circular ends joined by a curved surface

data: information that has been collected and can be compared

Frequency table	
Ladybirds	8
Beetles	6
Ants	11

day: a period of time that is 24 hours

denominator: the number of equal parts something has been divided into

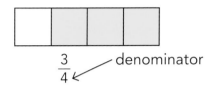

$\frac{3}{4}$ — denominator

diagonal: a straight line that goes from one corner to an opposite corner

difference: the result of a subtraction calculation

minuend − subtrahend = difference

$39 - 27 = 12$ — difference

digit: any of the symbols 0, 1, 2, 3, 4, 5, 6, 7, 8, 9

digital time: time written in numbers

divide, division: Split a whole into equal parts or share into equal parts. The symbol for divide is ÷.

dividend: the whole before it is divided

divisor: the number that you divide by

$6 \div \boxed{3} = 2$ — divisor

double: multiply by 2; a number becomes twice as large when it is doubled

●●● + ●●● = ●●●●●●

Double 3 is 3 + 3, which is 6

duration: how long something lasts

Swimming at
3 o'clock for 1 hour ←—duration

edge: a line where two faces of a solid shape meet

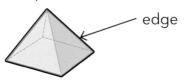
edge

equals: Has the same value. The symbol for equals is **=**.

equivalent: equal in quantity, size or value but might have a different appearance

$$\frac{1}{2} = \frac{2}{4}$$ 3 + 4 = 2 + 5

estimate: a rough answer to a question, found by making a thoughtful guess or rounding the numbers involved

estimating, estimation: deciding on a rough answer to a question, making a thoughtful guess or rounding the numbers involved

even number: a number that can be divided by 2 with nothing left over

exchange: changing one thing for another of equal value for example, 1 ten for 10 ones

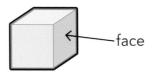

face: a flat surface of a 3-D shape

face

fact family: all the addition and subtraction calculations that can be made with one set of three numbers in a part–whole relationship

39	
12	27

12 + 27 = 39   39 – 12 = 27
39 = 12 + 27   27 = 39 – 12
27 + 12 = 39   39 – 27 = 12
39 = 27 + 12   12 = 39 – 27

factor: a number that divides exactly into another number

fewer than: a lower number than

formal written method: A method of adding or subtracting where the numbers are written vertically, according to the place value of each digit. Often called column method.

```
   2 6          5 4
 + 4 7        – 3 2
 -----        -----
   7 3          2 2
```

greater than (>): bigger in size or number

group: objects put together because they have something in common

half turn: A turn equal to two right angles. After a half turn you end up facing in the opposite direction from where you started.

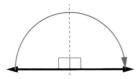

heptagon: a 2-D shape with 7 straight sides and 7 vertices

hexagon: a 2-D shape with 6 straight sides and 6 vertices

horizontal: at a right angle to the vertical, going side to side

hour: a period of time that is 60 minutes in length

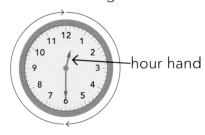

hour hand

hundreds column: the column on the left in a three-digit vertical calculation

$$\begin{array}{r} 5\ 6\ 7 \\ -\ 2\ 3\ 1 \\ \hline 3\ 3\ 6 \end{array}$$

hundreds number: a number that is a multiple of 100

100 200 300 400

inverse: An operation that reverses another operation. Addition is the inverse of subtraction; doubling is the inverse of halving.

$12 \div 3 = 4$ $4 \times 3 = 12$

leap year: A year that has 366 days, not a common year. Every 4th year is a leap year.

left over: the quantity remaining after division, also called the remainder

$21 \div 4 = 5\ r\ 1$ ← remainder

line model: a part–whole model diagram

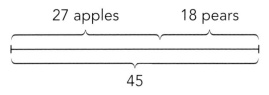

27 apples   18 pears

45

line of symmetry: a line through a shape that can be imagined or drawn, dividing it into two mirror-image halves

linked facts: information that is important for deciding what mathematics needs to be done when a problem is presented in words; the facts in a real-life situation which mean that we need to multiply or subtract etc.

magic square: a square filled with numbers so that all the rows, columns and diagonals have the same total

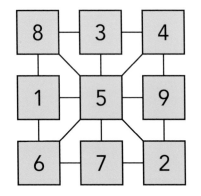

mental strategy: any method of working out the answer to a calculation in your head, without writing anything down

45 take away 6 equals 39 so I can use this to help!

450 – 60

method: a way of doing something

metre (m): unit of length equivalent to 100 cm

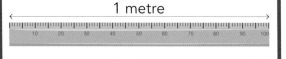

1 metre

metre stick: an instrument used to measure one metre

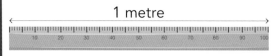

1 metre

millimetre (mm): a small unit of length; 10 mm is equivalent to 1 cm

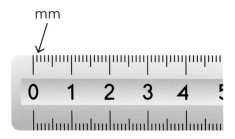

mm

minuend: the whole; the number being subtracted from; minuend – subtrahend = difference

14 – 10 = 4

minuend

minus: subtract

minute: A short period of time equivalent to 60 seconds. There are 60 minutes in an hour.

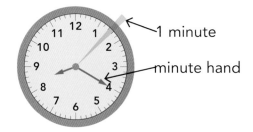

1 minute

minute hand

month: A period of time made up of at least 28 days. There are 12 months in every year.

May 2019						
S	M	T	W	T	F	S
			1	2	3	4
5	6	7	8	9	10	11
12	13	14	15	16	17	18
19	20	21	22	23	24	25
26	27	28	29	30	31	

multiple: when you multiply one whole number by another, the result is a multiple of the starting number; for example, the multiples of 5 are 5, 10, 15, 20, 25, 30, 35 and so on

$2 \times 3 = 6$
6 is a multiple of 2 and 3

multiplication grid: a list of multiples, usually of all the numbers 1 to 10 or 1 to 12

1	2	3	4	5	6	7	8	9	10
2	4	6	8	10	12	14	16	18	20
3	6	9	12	15	18	21	24	27	30
4	8	12	16	20	24	28	32	36	40
5	10	15	20	25	30	35	40	45	50
6	12	18	24	30	36	42	48	54	60
7	14	21	28	35	42	49	56	63	70
8	16	24	32	40	48	56	64	72	80
9	18	27	36	45	54	63	72	81	90
10	20	30	40	50	60	70	80	90	100

multiplication table: a list of multiplication sentences for one number up to × 12

$$3 \times 1 = 3$$
$$3 \times 2 = 6$$
$$3 \times 3 = 9$$
$$3 \times 4 = 12$$
$$3 \times 5 = 15$$
$$3 \times 6 = 18$$
$$3 \times 7 = 21$$
$$3 \times 8 = 24$$
$$3 \times 9 = 27$$
$$3 \times 10 = 30$$
$$3 \times 11 = 33$$
$$3 \times 12 = 36$$

multiply, multiplication: Repeat something a number of times or make it a number of times bigger. The symbol for multiply is ×.

non-unit fraction: a fraction in which the numerator is not 1

$$\frac{3}{4} \qquad \frac{7}{8}$$

number bond: pairs of numbers that make a whole

$$0 + 10 = 10$$
$$1 + 9 = 10$$
$$2 + 8 = 10$$
$$3 + 7 = 10$$
$$4 + 6 = 10$$
$$5 + 5 = 10$$
$$6 + 4 = 10$$
$$7 + 3 = 10$$
$$8 + 2 = 10$$
$$9 + 1 = 10$$
$$10 + 0 = 10$$

number line: a line of numbers in order, equally spaced and increasing in value from left to right towards infinity

0 1 2 3 4 5 6 7 8 9 10

number sentence: a mathematical sentence written with numerals and symbols

$$128 + 7 = 135$$

number sequence: a list of numbers that follow a certain rule or pattern

3, 6, 9, 12, 15, 18 …

numerator: the number of parts of an object, quantity or number that have been selected

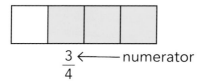

$$\frac{3}{4} \longleftarrow \text{numerator}$$

obtuse angle: An angle that is bigger than a right angle but smaller than a straight angle. It is greater than 90 degrees but less than 180 degrees.

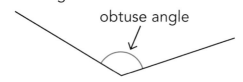

obtuse angle

octagon: a 2-D shape with 8 straight sides and 8 vertices

odd number: a number that cannot be divided exactly by 2; there is a remainder of 1

one(s): in a 2-digit number, the second digit shows the number of ones

67 ←ones

ones column: the column on the right in a vertical calculation, where the ones in each number are on top of each other

```
  5 6 7
- 2 3 1
  3 3 6
```

operation: a mathematical process, often +, −, × or ÷

---

p.m.: abbreviation for times between noon and midnight

parallel: lines that are side by side, the same distance apart and will never meet

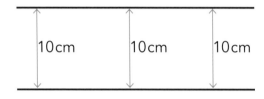

part: a portion or a segment of a whole

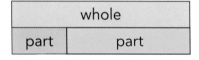

partition: split a number into 2 or more parts (often into 10s and 1s)

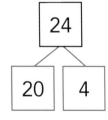

---

pattern: a regular arrangement of numbers or objects that follow a rule

pentagon: a 2-D shape with 5 straight sides and 5 vertices

perimeter: distance around the edge of a shape

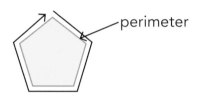

perimeter

perpendicular: lines that are at right angles to each other

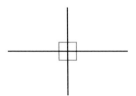

pictogram: a diagram to show information using pictures or symbols

| Monday | Tuesday | Wednesday |

 = 2 sweets

place value: the value of a digit depending on its place or position in a number

tens ones
35

place value arrow cards: a set of place value cards with an arrow on the right hand side that is lined up to make the number

569

place value chart: a chart with columns labelled to show hundreds, tens and ones

Hundreds	Tens	Ones

place value stick abacus: an abacus with the sticks labelled to show hundreds, tens and ones

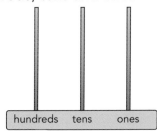

hundreds   tens   ones

placeholder: a zero is a number that has no value itself

plus: add

$+$

polygon: a 2-D shape with 3 or more straight sides

prism: a 3-D shape with two identical ends and flat faces

product: the answer when two numbers are multiplied together

$12 \times 6 = 72$ ← product

pyramid: a 3-D shape with a polygon base and triangular faces that meet at the top (apex)

quadrilateral: a 2-D shape with 4 straight sides and 4 vertices

quantity: a number of objects or an amount of something

quarter turn: a turn equal to one right angle

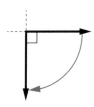

quotient: when a number is divided by another number, the answer is the quotient

$72 \div 12 = 6$ ← quotient

recombine: put numbers back together after partitioning

rectangle: A 2-D shape with 4 straight sides and 4 vertices. Opposite sides are equal in length.

regrouping: re-partition tens and ones to help with calculating

Regrouping

remainder: the amount that is left over after a division when another equal group cannot be made

$$13 \div 4 = 3 \, r \, 1$$

repeated addition: adding the same value repeatedly

repeated subtraction: subtracting the same value repeatedly

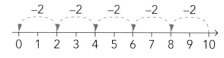

right angle: a quarter turn

Roman numeral: number written with symbols from the Roman times

IV, V, VI, IX, X, XI

rotate: turn an object around a fixed point

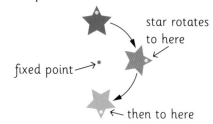

star rotates to here

fixed point →

← then to here

round, rounding: to make a number simpler by writing the nearest tens number or hundreds number instead

nearest 10

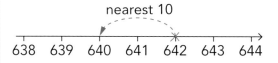

row: an arrangement of numbers or objects placed side by side, or horizontally

ruler: an instrument used to measure lengths in millimetres, centimetres and metres

second: a very short period of time; there are 60 seconds in a minute

side: the line joining two vertices of a 2-D shape

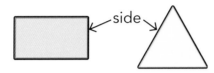

single-digit number: A number with only one digit. These are the numbers less than 10.

solution: the answer to a calculation or problem

sphere: a 3-D shape that is perfectly round like a ball

square: A 2-D shape with 4 straight sides and 4 vertices. All sides are the same length.

square number: a number obtained when a whole number is multiplied by itself

$$5 \times 5 = 25, \text{ so } 25 \text{ is a square number}$$

statistical table: a table containing data

Frequency table	
Ladybirds	8
Beetles	6
Ants	11

statistics: data; numerical facts that give information about something

Frequency table	
Ladybirds	⑧
Beetles	⑥
Ants	⑪

◁ statistics

subtract, subtraction: Find the difference between two numbers. The symbol for subtract is –.

subtrahend: the number (27) being subtracted from the minuend; minuend – subtrahend = difference

$$39 - ㉗ = 12$$ ← subtrahend

sum: the total of an addition calculation

$$12 + 2 = ⑭$$ ← sum

survey: a way of collecting data by asking people questions or observing something

symmetrical: having symmetry

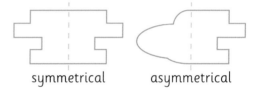

symmetrical   asymmetrical

symmetry: a shape has symmetry when one half is a mirror image of the other half

mirror line

tally: a way to count things in sets (of 5) using lines to represent numbers

tally chart: a chart that uses tally marks to show how many of each thing

Tally chart	
Ladybirds	卌 |||
Beetles	卌	
Ants	卌 卌	

---

ten frame: a 5 by 2 grid

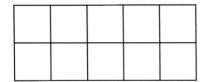

---

tens column: the second column from the right in a vertical calculation

```
  5 6 7
− 2 3 1
─────
  3 3 6
```

---

tens number: a number that is a multiple of 10

1	2	3	4	5	6	7	8	9	10
11	12	13	14	15	16	17	18	19	20
21	22	23	24	25	26	27	28	29	30
31	32	33	34	35	36	37	38	39	40
41	42	43	44	45	46	47	48	49	50
51	52	53	54	55	56	57	58	59	60
61	62	63	64	65	66	67	68	69	70
71	72	73	74	75	76	77	78	79	80
81	82	83	84	85	86	87	88	89	90
91	92	93	94	95	96	97	98	99	100

---

tenth: when something is divided into ten equal parts, each one of them is one tenth

← one tenth

---

three-digit number: a number that has three digits (these are between 100 and 999)

---

three dimensional (3-D): A shape is 3 dimensional if it has length, width and height. A cube is an example of a 3-D shape.

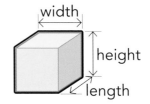

width
height
length

---

three-quarter turn: If I am facing 12 on the clock and make a three-quarter turn in a clockwise direction, I will be facing 9. Making a turn of 3 right angles.

---

times: another word for multiply

$$2 \times 6 = 12$$

---

total: another word for sum; the result of addition

$12 + 2 = (14)$ ← total

---

total price: the total cost of all items

---

triangle: a 2-D shape with 3 straight sides and 3 angles

triangular-based prism: a 3-D shape with two triangular ends and 3 rectangular sides

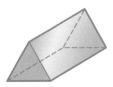

two dimensional (2-D): A shape that has only two dimensions, width and length, and no depth or thickness. These can only be seen on paper or on a screen.

unit fraction: a fraction in which the numerator is 1

$$\frac{1}{2} \qquad \frac{1}{4} \qquad \frac{1}{10}$$

unit price: what one item costs

vertex: a point where two or more straight lines meet (2-D shapes) or 3 or more faces meet (3-D shapes)

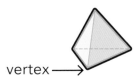

vertex ⟶

vertical: In an up and down direction. A table leg is vertical.

vertices: More than one vertex. This tetrahedron has 4 vertices.

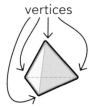

vertices

week: a period of time made up of 7 days

			May 2019			
S	M	T	W	T	F	S
			1	2	3	4
5	6	7	8	9	10	11
12	13	14	15	16	17	18
19	20	21	22	23	24	25
26	27	28	29	30	31	

whole: sum of the parts

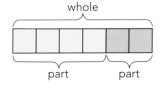

whole

part   part

written method: any method of working out the answer to a calculation in writing

$$546 + 300 = 846$$
$$846 + 30 = 876$$
$$876 + 9 = 885$$
so $\quad 546 + 339 = 885$

year: a period of time made up of 12 months

2020 Calendar

zero: The number before 1 in our number system. Zero has no value.

1	2	3	4	5	6	7	8	9	10
11	12	13	14	15	16	17	18	19	20
21	22	23	24	25	26	27	28	29	30
31	32	33	34	35	36	37	38	39	40
41	42	43	44	45	46	47	48	49	50
51	52	53	54	55	56	57	58	59	60
61	62	63	64	65	66	67	68	69	70
71	72	73	74	75	76	77	78	79	80
81	82	83	84	85	86	87	88	89	90
91	92	93	94	95	96	97	98	99	100